D0943795

BOOKWORMS

Tools We Use
Artists

Instrumentos de trabajo
Los artistas

Dana Meachen Rau

mc Marshall Cavendish
Benchmark
New York

CSCL

What are all these colors for?

An artist is ready to start painting.

---❖---

¿Para qué son todos estos colores?

Un artista está listo para empezar a pintar.

Paint comes in tubes, jars, or cans.

Brushes come in many shapes and sizes.

La pintura viene en tubos, frascos o latas.

Los pinceles vienen en muchas formas y tamaños.

The artist dips his brush in the paint.

An *easel* holds the picture while he paints.

❖

El artista moja su pincel en la pintura.

Un *caballete* sostiene el cuadro mientras él pinta.

Some artists draw with pencils.
Some use colorful chalk.

—————◆—————

Algunas artistas dibujan con lápices.
Algunas usan tizas de colores.

Some artists make *collages*.
They glue down bits of paper.

❖

Algunas artistas hacen *collages*.
Pegan trocitos de papel.

Some artists do not need paper.
They sew with cloth and thread.

———————◆———————

Algunas artistas no necesitan papel.
Cosen con tela e hilo.

Artists also make *sculptures*.

An artist shapes clay with his hands.

❖

Los artistas también hacen *esculturas*.

Un artista modela la arcilla con las manos.

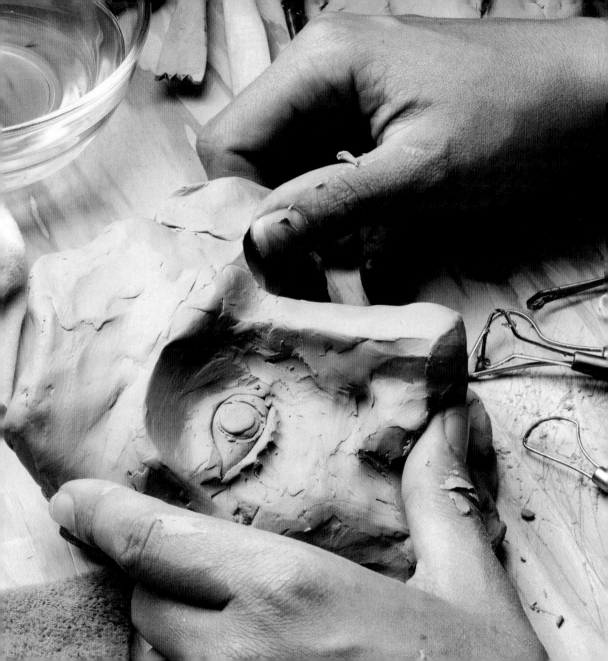

He spins the clay on a wheel.

He cuts the clay with a knife.

❖

Él hace girar la arcilla en
un torno.

Corta la arcilla con un cuchillo.

Some artists work with metal.

They use fire to melt and join the parts.

Algunos artistas trabajan con metal.

Usan fuego para fundir y unir las piezas.

A sculpture can be made
of stone.

An artist breaks off pieces with
a *chisel*.

———————❖———————

Una escultura se puede hacer
en piedra.

Un artista parte trozos de la
piedra con un *cincel*.

An artist can use wood to make a sculpture.

He carves the wood with a knife.

❖

Un artista puede usar madera para hacer una escultura.

Talla la madera con un cuchillo.

You can be an artist.

You can draw a picture with crayons.

Tú puedes ser artista.

Puedes hacer un dibujo con creyones.

You can make a sculpture with paper, paste, and paint.

Imagination is your most important tool.

———————❖———————

Puedes hacer una escultura con papel, pegamento y pintura.

La imaginación es tu instrumento de trabajo más importante.

Tools Artists Use
Instrumentos de trabajo de los artistas

brushes
pinceles

chisel
cincel

easel
caballete

knife
cuchillo

28

| **paint** | **pencil** | **wheel** |
| **pintura** | **lápiz** | **torno** |

Challenge Words

chisel A tool used to chip stone.

collages Pictures made of pieces of paper or other items glued together.

easel A stand that holds a painting.

sculptures Art that is shaped out of wood, stone, metal, clay, or wax.

Vocabulario avanzado

cincel Instrumento que se usa para partir trozos de piedra.

collages Cuadros que se hacen pegando trocitos de papel u otros elementos.

caballete Base donde se coloca una pintura.

esculturas Trabajo artístico que se hace con madera, piedra, metal, arcilla o cera.

29

Index

Índice

About the Author

Dana Meachen Rau is an author, editor, and illustrator. A graduate of Trinity College in Hartford, Connecticut, she has written more than one hundred fifty books for children, including nonfiction, biographies, early readers, and historical fiction. She lives with her family in Burlington, Connecticut.

With thanks to the Reading Consultants:

Nanci Vargus, Ed.D., is an Assistant Professor of Elementary Education at the University of Indianapolis.

Beth Walker Gambro received her M.S. Ed. Reading from the University of St. Francis, Joliet, Illinois.

Sobre la autora

Dana Meachen Rau es escritora, editora e ilustradora. Graduada del Trinity College de Hartford, Connecticut, ha escrito más de ciento cincuenta libros para niños, entre ellos libros de ficción histórica y de no ficción, biografías y libros de lectura para principiantes. Vive con su familia en Burlington, Connecticut.

Con agradecimiento a las asesoras de lectura:

Nanci R. Vargus, Dra. en Ed., es profesora ayudante de educación primaria en la Universidad de Indianápolis.

Beth Walker Gambro recibió su Maestría en Ciencias de la Educación, con especialización en Lectura, de la Universidad de St. Francis, en Joliet, Illinois.

Marshall Cavendish Benchmark
99 White Plains Road
Tarrytown, New York 10591-9001
www.marshallcavendish.us

Library of Congress Cataloging-in-Publication Data

Rau, Dana Meachen, 1971–
Artists / by Dana Meachen Rau = Los artistas / de Dana Meachen Rau.
p. cm. – (Bookworms. Tools we use = los Instrumentos de trabajo)
English and Spanish.
Includes index.
ISBN 978-0-7614-2820-6 (bilingual edition) – ISBN 978-0-7614-2796-4 (Spanish edition)
ISBN 978-0-7614-2655-4 (English edition)
1. Artists' tools–Juvenile literature. 2. Artists' materials–Juvenile literature.
I. Title. II. Title: Los artistas.
N8543.R39 2007
702.8–dc22
2007013905

Spanish Translation and Text Composition by
Victory Productions, Inc.

Photo Research by Anne Burns Images

Cover Photo by *SuperStock*/Roger Allyn Lee

The photographs in this book are used with permission and through the courtesy of:
SuperStock: pp. 1, 17, 29R age fotostock; p. 15 SuperStock. *Corbis*: pp. 3, 29L Corbis;
pp. 5, 28TL Gregor Schuster/zefa; pp. 7, 28BL Ashley Cooper; pp. 9, 29C Patrick Ward;
p. 11 Gabe Palmer/zefa; p. 19 Layne Kennedy; pp. 21, 23, 28TR, 28BR Peter Beck;
p. 25 Laura Dwight; p. 27 Jose Luis Pelaez, Inc.
Woodfin Camp: p. 13 John Eastcott & Yva Momatiuk.

Printed in Malaysia
1   3   5   6   4   2

DATE DUE